W9-BXP-978

Do-It-Yourself
FRAMED QUILTS
Fast, Fun & Easy Projects

Gai Perry

C&T PUBLISHING

©2001 Gai Perry

Front Cover: Clockwise from top: *Concentric Diamonds, Sunlight, Hollyhocks, Dragonfly Creek, Field of Flowers.* Photo styling by John Vitale.
Back Cover: *Chintzware Plates, Meadow Stream.*

Editor: Candie Frankel
Technical Editor: Carolyn Aune
Copy Editor: Carol Barrett
Design Director: Diane Pedersen
Production Assistants: Stephanie Muir, Tim Manibusan
Book Designer: Rohani Design
Quilt Photographer: Sharon Risedorph
Framing Chapter Photographer: Rich Perry
Author Photographer: Diane Pederson
Illustrator: Tim Manibusan
Cover Designer: Kristen Yenche

Published by C&T Publishing, Inc. P.O. Box 1456, Lafayette, California 94549

All rights reserved. No part of this work covered by the copyright hereon may be reproduced or used in any form or by any means—graphic, electronic, or mechanical, including photocopying, recording, taping, or information storage and retrieval systems—without written permission of the publisher. Quilt block patterns designed by the author may be copied for personal use. Credit should be printed on every copy made. Historic traditional block patterns are in the public domain and are not restricted by this copyright. The copyrights on individual artworks are retained by the artists as noted in *Do-It-Yourself Framed Quilts.*

Exception: The author and publisher give permission to photocopy a maximum of two copies each of pages 63, 77, and 78 for personal use only.

Attention Teachers:
C&T Publishing, Inc. encourages you to use this book as a text for teaching. Contact us at 800-284-1114 or www.ctpub.com for more information about the C&T Teachers Program.

We take great care to ensure that the information included in this book is accurate and presented in good faith, but no warranty is provided nor results guaranteed. Since we have no control over the choice of materials or procedures used, neither the author nor C&T Publishing, Inc. shall have any liability to any person or entity with respect to any loss or damage caused directly or indirectly by the information contained in this book.

Trademarked™ and Registered Trademarked® names are used throughout this book. Rather than use the symbols with every occurrence of a trademark and registered trademark name, we are using the names only in an editorial fashion and to the benefit of the owner, with no intention of infringement.

Library of Congress Cataloging-in-Publication Data

Perry, Gai,
Do-it-yourself framed quilts : fast, fun & easy projects / by Gai Perry.
   p. cm.
    ISBN 1-57120-174-2 (paper trade)
    1. Patchwork—Patterns. 2. Miniature quilts. 3. Wall hangings.
  4. Fabric pictures. 5. Picture frames and framing. I. Title.
TT835 . P3522 2001
746.46'041--dc21

                                                      2001001984

Printed in Singapore
10 9 8 7 6 5 4 3 2 1

CONTENTS

PREFACE

One crisp October afternoon, I received a phone call from a former student of mine named Merrie Powell. After the opening pleasantries like "How have you been?" and "What are you working on?" she asked if I would give her permission to teach from my second book, *Impressionist Palette*. In particular, she wanted to offer a class on the *Victorian Bouquet* pattern—but her idea was to teach a much smaller version of it, practically a miniature.

It was very thoughtful of Merrie to ask, and of course I said yes, but after I hung up the phone I felt a little tingle of jealousy. Making small Impressionist quilts that could be nicely framed without spending a small fortune was something I'd been wanting to try for years, but just hadn't gotten around to.

Bouquet for Gai, 14" × 14",
by Merrie Powell

Oh, well. I was in the middle of a busy teaching schedule and soon forgot about it. Then, two weeks later, a package arrived in the mail. Merrie had sent me one of her small bouquet quilts, and it was *fabulous.* Believe me, there is nothing like a little one-upmanship to stir the creative juices. I practically flew into my sewing room and started cutting out squares for one of *my own* small quilts.

Over the next three months, in occasional odd moments between Thanksgiving, Christmas, and a horrendous January flu bug, I made and framed several little landscape quilts. I even made a few traditional and contemporary pieces. They could be designed and sewn so quickly and were such a pleasure to make, I found myself becoming addicted! At first, I designed them strictly for my own enjoyment, and perhaps to sell, but gradually it occurred to me that if I was having this much fun, why not share it?

So, surprise, Merrie! I'm dedicating this book to you for nudging me toward the kind of quilts I've always wanted to make and for inadvertently inspiring the concept for this book. I will be forever grateful!

INTRODUCTION

From the gray-green waters of the Atlantic to the blue-green waters of the Pacific, Americans have a mind-set that says bigger is better (I think it must be built into our gene pool). Quilters are no exception. The bigger the quilts, the more impressed we are. We ooh! and aah! over them at quilt shows, and they invariably win the blue ribbons.

But in the reality of daily living, how many of us have the time it requires to make large quilts? For most of us, our creative minutes are so precious, and we have so many ideas to pursue, that we end up making smaller quilts. Unfortunately, smaller quilts, no matter how wonderful they are, often end up looking like glorified potholders or placemats. Something needs to be added to these small quilts to give them the importance they deserve. And that something is framing.

Put a carefully selected mat and frame around a small quilt, hang it on the wall, and instantly it becomes ART!

Personally, I love small quilts, and making one can be every bit as creative as painting a picture. Because of the diminutive size, the placement of every square and triangle becomes vitally important, and just like an artist, the quilter must keep arranging and rearranging her color and value contrasts until some inner vision is satisfied. The good thing is that with a small quilt, this agony-ecstasy process can be accomplished in a matter of hours, not days or weeks. Think of the possibilities for decorating your home or for gift giving.

Between the covers of *Do-It-Yourself Framed Quilts* you are going to find all sorts of helpful information about designing small quilts and framing them yourself using precut mats and ready-made frames, or framing strips, to keep the cost down. And incidentally, you're going to be blissfully surprised when you find out how inexpensive ready-made framing is when compared to custom framing.

Whether you prefer contemporary, traditional, or pictorial quilts, I invite you to put yourself in the mind of an artist where colors are brighter, images are clearer, and the intent is to create a little magic for your walls.

SAMPLER OF FRAME STYLES

*T*here is an extensive gallery of framed quilts starting on page 33, but just to whet your appetite, here are six different and effective ways to frame a quilt. Once you have mastered the simple framing techniques described on pages 67–73, I'm sure you will discover a whole world of framing possibilities. How about framing a delicate lace handkerchief from your grandmother's era, or a special matchbook collection that once belonged to your great-uncle Harry. With ready-made frames, if it doesn't move, you can frame it!

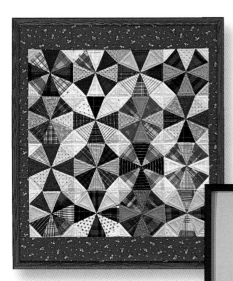

▶
Pink and Yellow Roses, Gai Perry, Frame and Mat Size: 16" × 20"
This rose bouquet quilt is surrounded by a simple, yet elegant, ready-made silver and gold frame. I think the double-layer green mat is the perfect color to accent the vase.

▲
Scrap Kaleidoscope, Gai Perry, Frame Size: 26" × 30"
The Kaleidoscope block is one of my favorite quilt patterns. It's easy to sew, yet the optical illusion created by alternating the light and dark pie shapes is intriguing. I chose tobacco-colored oak framing strips to enhance this traditional-style quilt. To reproduce the quilt, make sixteen 6" (finished size) blocks.

◀
Feathered Star, Gai Perry, Frame and Mat Size: 16" × 16"
This is one of my early "learning-to-piece" quilts. You know, the kind you throw in a drawer and forget. Here it is, resurrected and framed. I splurged and had the mat and frame custom-made, but I did the mounting myself to save labor charges.

▶
Pot of Posies, Gai Perry, Frame and Mat Size: 16" x 20"
I found the perfect shiny red wooden frame for this luscious bouquet quilt. I think the white and green double-layer mat lends an added sparkle. The red plaid tablecloth gives the quilt a country feeling, and I know it's going to look terrific hanging against the red, green, and cream striped wallpaper in my kitchen.

▲
Art Nouveau, Gai Perry, Frame and Mat Size: 14" x 11"
I bought this art nouveau fabric print because I loved it, but I couldn't figure out what to do with it. The final solution was to make it into a "whole-cloth" quilt and then frame it—perfect when you need a gift in a hurry. The ready-made carved gilt frame is called a "gallery" style.

▶
Positive-Negative, Gai Perry,
Frame and Mat Size: 16" × 20"
Black metal framing strips complement the hard-edge look of this contemporary-style quilt design. I like the way the mat cuts off the edges of the quilt. One might assume that it is a segment from a much larger piece. The quilt was made with 2½" (finished size) blocks.

LET'S GET STARTED

*I*n keeping with the easy, fast, fun theme of *Do-It-Yourself Framed Quilts,* most of the patterns in this book are simple combinations of squares and triangles. Because the quilts are small, they can be designed quickly and are a breeze to sew.

Here is a short list of design tools followed by a brief discussion of three design priorities that can help you to create some spectacular quilt pictures. Please don't skip over this section!

Design Tools

The best design tools you own are your eyes to observe and your intellect to process what you see. They don't cost anything, and they come beautifully packaged. You will also need:

- Transparent template plastic
- Scissors (to cut template plastic)
- Sharp fabric-cutting scissors
- Rotary cutter and mat
- White Chaco-Liner (to mark dark fabrics)
- Black permanent-ink fine-point pen (to mark light fabrics)
- Omnigrid® ruler or similar style marked in ¼" increments (for rotary cutting and measuring)
- 1 yard of Steam-A-Seam 2®
- Fabric paints such as Setacolor® or artists' acrylics (optional)
- 1 yard of 44"- to 45"-wide white cotton flannel
- Design Board (see instructions on page 9)

I'm going to be a little bossy for a moment and insist that your cutting implements are sharp. I go crazy watching a student attempt to cut fabric with scissors that are so dull, they couldn't cut a straight line through butter. Don't laugh. If you recognize yourself, please have your scissors sharpened, or treat yourself to a new pair. You'll save yourself hours of frustration. No dull pencils either. They make too thick a line for accurate piecing. When it becomes necessary to trace around a template, use a black permanent ink pen or a white Chaco-Liner.

How to Make a Design Board

All the quilts in this book start their life on a design board. To make a design board, purchase a piece of foam-core board that measures 32" × 40" or 40" × 60". Foam-core is available at craft, office, and art supply stores. Pin the yard of white cotton flannel to the foam-core. (Note: If you put some pins along all four edges of the flannel, it will lie smooth and flat and pieces of fabric will adhere to it without the need for additional pinning. If the flannel is larger than your foam-core, either cut it down or fold it over the edges of the board and secure it to the back side with pins.) Now lean your completed design board against a wall or some other support that will keep it in an upright position and you're ready to start your first masterpiece.

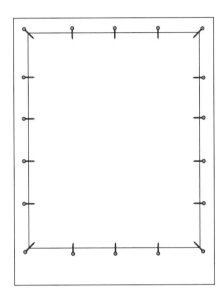

Flannel-Lined Design Board

Three Design Priorities

> *"Art . . . should simplify. That, indeed is very nearly the whole of the higher artistic process; finding what conventions of form and detail one can do without and yet preserve the spirit of the whole."*
> —Willa Cather, 1920

1. SIMPLIFY YOUR DESIGN

The words of author Willa Cather eloquently express my approach to designing quilts that are destined to hang on a wall. The key word is *simplify*. Simplify the content of the design; take out all the extraneous elements. Choose brilliant combinations of color and fabric patterns, then let them do the work of capturing the viewer's attention. Keep these thoughts in mind and you will find that making a framed quilt can be an artistic and pleasurable experience. And here are some added perks: You don't have to mass-produce a hundred or so formula-size units, and you don't have to wrestle with a growing quilt top as it becomes cumbersome and awkward to handle. Instead, you can concentrate on creating a small jewel of a piece where every square and triangle plays a vital role in the overall design.

2. SAY YES TO TEMPLATES!

Because each piece of fabric makes a vital contribution to the finished design, it often becomes necessary to use templates instead of strip-cutting the squares. Using a template removes the hit-or-miss factor and allows you to choose just the right section of fabric to enhance your design. When you start working on one of the Impressionist patterns, you will see just how necessary templates are. (For more information on "fussy-cutting," see pages 15–16.)

3. ESTABLISH CONTRASTS!

When you first look at a quilt, your initial response is to the colors. Next, you assess the subject matter, and finally, the quality of the workmanship. You probably don't consciously think about contrast, but if you did, you'd recognize that it is frequently the effective use of contrast, not the colors or subject matter, that makes a quilt memorable.

Contrast is especially important when you are making a quilt to frame and hang on the wall. You want to catch the viewer's attention from across the room, so with each pattern you attempt, make a conscious effort to incorporate at least three kinds of contrast. In quilt design, the following contrasts are particularly effective.

Contrast of Warm and Cool Colors. This is the easiest contrast to achieve. All you have to do is mix some warm colors (reds, oranges, yellows) with some cool colors (blues, greens, and purples). If you want an even stronger effect, consider using the *contrast of complements,* which is the pairing of colors that are opposite each other on the color circle: red and green, yellow and purple, orange and blue.

Contrast of Value. Every quilt you make should contain some light-, medium-, and dark-value fabrics. It's the combination of these three values that gives each of them more definition. Many of us seem to gravitate toward medium-value prints. I bet if you were to organize your fabric collection into three value piles, one for light, one for medium, and one for dark, you would find the medium-value pile much larger. Think about gradually adding some interesting light and dark prints to your fabric collection.

Contrast of Saturation. This simply means pairing pure bright colors with colors that have been toned down or that look dull by comparison. It's a subtle contrast that will give your quilt a glowing richness.

I made this quilt, *Study in Contrast,* back in 1989. Aptly named, it incorporates just about all of the contrast elements I've just been discussing.

Contrast of Print Scale. Scale means the size of the print repeat. Please don't fall into the trap of choosing prints that all have the same print scale. Use a mixture of small-, medium-, and large-scale prints to create movement.

Contrast of Fabric Personality. This contrast refers to the nature of the fabric design: plaid, solid, floral, stripe, etc. Here again, mix them up for more visual interest.

Contrast of Quilting Pattern. When the design of a quilt is crisp and uncluttered, use some intricate quilting patterns for, you guessed it, contrast. Simple design, fancy stitching. Love it!

DESIGN PRIORITIES SUMMATION

1. Keep the design simple. Use spectacular fabrics and color combinations to attract the viewer's attention.
2. Accept the fact that you are going to have to use templates and do some "fussy-cutting."
3. Put at least three kinds of contrast into each quilt picture.

Island Inlet, Gai Perry, 35" × 40"
This is the original Island Inlet
quilt that became the inspiration
for Pattern Five (page 30).

IMPRESSIONIST QUILTS

I started making quilts in 1981, and three years later no one was more surprised than I to find myself teaching "traditional color" to quilters who probably had far more sewing skills than I possessed. But I loved making quilts, so I can only hope my enthusiasm made up for my lack of technical proficiency. In spite of my earlier seat-of-the-pants teaching style, working with color has always been my abiding passion, and I'm sure it was my painting background that led me to make my first Impressionist quilt.

I developed the Impressionist quilting technique in 1990, and I have been refining it ever since. At first, I was pure of heart, content to make my quilt pictures without any kind of embellishment. Those days are long gone! Now I'll show you how to use paint and Steam-A-Seam 2 fusible webbing to enhance your designs.

If you're bitten by the Impressionist quilt bug after making a few small pieces and want to try something larger, you'll find patterns and extensive design information in two of my other books, *Impressionist Quilts* and *Impressionist Palette* (see Reference Books on page 79).

~

Design Basics

Impressionism is a painting style that interprets individual elements with warm-cool color contrasts and value changes in order to attain a luminous impression of the whole. The results are softened outlines allowing one area of a picture to blend into another without hard edges. You are going to create the same romantic effect with fabric.

Before you start working on your first Impressionist pattern, I'd like to acquaint you with a few design basics that apply to all the patterns in this section. Individual design issues are addressed with each pattern.

2¼" Base Square. All the Impressionist quilt pictures are made with a combination of squares and triangles. The base square—the pattern piece most frequently used— measures 2¼". Occasionally, a pattern will require the use of a smaller or larger square or rectangle. Triangles measuring 2⅝" are used around the perimeter to render the quilt "in-square."

On-Point Orientation. All the squares are positioned on-point and are sewn into diagonal rows rather than straight rows. I've found that placing the squares on-point creates a more effective illusion of blending. In my opinion, pictorial quilts with straight rows of squares tend to look like digital printouts.

Templates. In many instances, the fabric squares and triangles are cut individually, using templates. This method ensures getting just the right section of fabric for your quilt picture. The Impressionist quilt template patterns can be found on page 77.

Back of the Fabric. Always consider using the back, or reverse side, of a fabric. It is usually softer in color and can help to create a smoother blend from one color area to another.

Diagonal Grid. If you have trouble following the Design Diagram which is included with each pattern, try drawing a 2¼" diagonal grid on your flannel design board. See page 17 for instructions.

Sizing. Four of the five Impressionist quilt patterns in this book are designed to fit a 16" × 20" mat and frame. I chose this size because it is the largest ready-made frame available that also has a good assortment of corresponding 16" × 20" precut mats. The patterns are designed to be larger than the mat openings to account for shrinkage after quilting and to allow enough excess to secure it under the mat.

Fabric Information

ELEMENT PRINTS

When I first developed the Impressionist quilt technique, I had to combine several tone-on-tone and textured prints to create the illusion of elements like grass, water, trees, and sky. Now, thanks to the fabric industry's astute ability in reading quilting

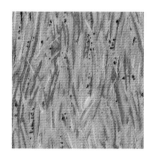

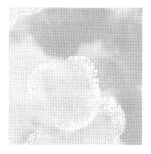

Grass   Water   Trees   Sky

trends, we have a wondrous selection of element prints: Grasses that look real enough to mow, water shimmering with sunlight, trees blowing in a gentle breeze, and skies with fluffy clouds. As if that weren't enough, each print usually comes in an assortment of colorways. The result is that I've been able to design a collection of small Impressionist quilt patterns that use as few as three or four fabrics each.

FLORAL PRINTS

The elements I've just been talking about (grass, water, trees, and sky) are generally interpreted with cool colors, just as they are in nature. The addition of flowers will provide the warm contrast and become the focal point of your quilt picture. Floral prints with medium-dark and dark backgrounds are more effective than those with light backgrounds because the colors of the flowers are generally more intense. Also, try not to combine light and dark background floral prints in the same quilt. If you do, once the quilt is sewn, wherever a light background square appears, it will look like a hole in the quilt.

Ideally, the flower or flowers should fill the square, allowing most of the background to disappear into the seam allowance. Some patterns call for smaller-scale wildflowers while others require a larger individual flower to fill a 2¼" or 4" square. All the floral prints you consider using should have leaves. Florals without leaves look unnatural and are difficult to combine with other floral prints.

One flower fills a 2¼" square

Smaller field flowers

Cutting Methods

CUTTING FLORAL PRINT SQUARES WITH A TEMPLATE

Move the see-through plastic template around a floral print fabric until you find an image that pleases you. Because all the squares are set on-point, it is necessary to position the flowers so they are growing toward a point of the template. Don't worry about cutting off-grain; concentrate on getting the flower to look like it is growing naturally toward the sky.

Once the template is in place, trace around the perimeter with a black permanent ink pen or a white Chaco-Liner. Then cut out the square of fabric with your new or newly sharpened scissors. (Note: If you prefer, you can omit tracing around the template and use your rotary cutter to cut out the square of fabric. You will probably have to make a new template each time the old one gets accidentally sliced.)

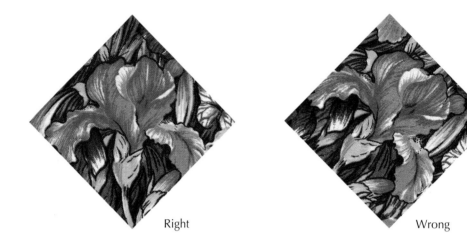

Right   Wrong

STRIP-CUTTING ELEMENT PRINT SQUARES

I like to cut out element print squares by hand so that I have complete control of what goes into the quilt. But if you feel the need to exercise your rotary cutter (or you're experiencing rotary-withdrawal), you can cut element prints for grass, water, tree, and sky areas into 2¼" strips and then into 2¼" squares.

Now this is important! In many element print fabrics, the motifs or textures are printed across the grain, from selvage to selvage. Because the squares for Impressionist quilts are set on-point, you must cut the 2¼" strips at a 45° angle. Use the 45° cutting line on your rotary cutting mat. If the direction of the print isn't a factor, strips may be cut on the straight grain.

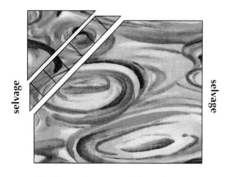

Cutting strips at a 45° angle

Cutting strips on the straight grain

Design Enhancement

Once your Impressionist quilt picture is sewn, you should critique it to decide if, or how, it can be improved. Sometimes a little touch-up paint is needed, or maybe some additional flowers and leaves.

I used to appliqué little fabric additions, but now I use Steam-A-Seam 2, a fusible webbing that can do instant wonders for a quilt picture. What I like about Steam-A-Seam 2 is that after you finger-press a flower or leaf to the top side of the fusible webbing, cut it out, and peel off the protective backing paper, there is enough stickiness to allow it to temporarily adhere to your quilt top. This gives you the opportunity to move the flower or leaf around until you find the perfect spot for it. Then heat-press according to the package directions.

How to Draw a Diagonal Grid

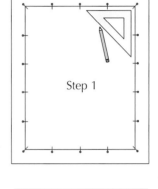

Step 1

Step 1: After you have pinned a piece of white flannel to your design board, place a drafting triangle on the upper right-hand corner (longest side facing toward the center of the flannel) and draw a pencil line.

Step 2: Use a ruler (a) to continue drawing diagonal lines that measure 2¼" apart across the surface of the flannel (b).

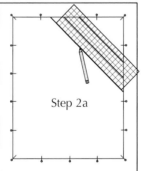

Step 2a

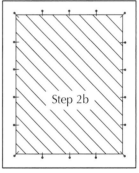

Step 2b

Step 3: To make the diagonal lines going in the opposing direction, place the ruler across the upper left-hand corner of the flannel. Line up the 2¼" increment marks on the ruler with the pencil lines on the flannel and draw a diagonal line. Continue drawing diagonal lines that measure 2¼" apart across the flannel.

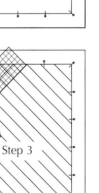

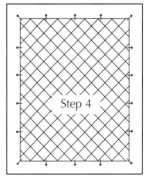

Step 3

Step 4

Step 4: The finished grid.

PATTERN ONE

Meadow Stream by Gai Perry

Frame and Mat Size: 16" × 20"

Meadow Stream is designed to look like a close-up photo of a shallow stream meandering through a meadow. It should be easy to make, but its ultimate success depends upon selecting water, grass, and flower prints that "color-blend." Effective color blending happens when one area of the composition moves into the next without obvious color changes. The pattern quilt pairs a rich blue water print with some tall blue-green grass. They are enhanced by a sprinkling of bright yellow and blue flowers.

Your finished quilt will be as good as your ability to select fabrics, and hopefully, there will be plenty of options at your local quilt store. You could choose a luminous gray-green water print and pair it with a gray-green grass print. Then, for contrast, add any color of bright flowers you like—just make sure the leaves on the flowers are the same hue as the water and grass. You could also think about doing the scene in fall colors. Start with an elegant mahogany and rust-colored batik for the water, then choose vibrant tones of red, gold, and brown for the flowers and grass. Yummy!

Fabric Categories and Quantities

Water: ¼ yard of one print that gives the impression of moving water. It should be streaked with light- and dark-value areas to suggest reflecting sunlight.

Tall Grass: ¼ yard of one element print that looks like grass that is growing wild. The grass should be in the same color family as the water. If you can't find an appropriate grass print, eliminate this element from your quilt and cut additional squares from the transition flowers print.

Transition Flowers: ⅓ yard of one floral print with small, colorful flowers and leaves that blend with the color of the water and the grass.

Larger Flowers: ⅓ yard of one floral print that gives the feeling of flowers growing wild in a meadow. These flowers should be slightly larger than the transition flowers. Choose a print with light or bright flowers to provide contrast with the water and grass. Make sure the leaves and the background blend with the color of the water and grass.

Method

Before you begin, be sure to read pages 13–16 for information on how to go about cutting squares from prints such as water and flowers. The Meadow Stream Design Diagram (page 20) is your guide to the placement of the squares, but nothing is written in stone, so feel free to make changes.

Step 1: Cut twenty-eight 2¼" water print squares and five 2⅝" water print triangles for the perimeter. Position the pieces on your design board. Try to create areas of light reflection and shadow. The lightest-value water squares should appear in the middle of the stream. (Note: As you cut the perimeter triangles, think about the directional flow of the water.)

Step 2: Cut and place twelve 2¼" grass print squares and three 2⅝" grass print perimeter triangles on your design board.

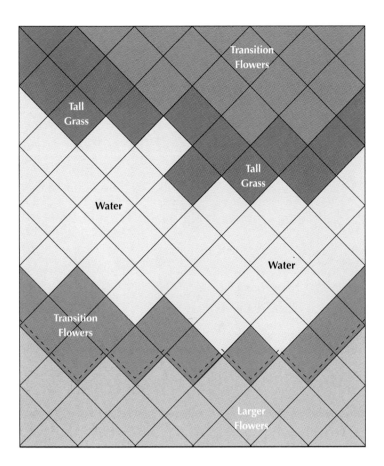

Step 3: Cut and place twenty 2¼" transition floral print squares and eight 2⅝" transition floral print perimeter triangles on your design board.

Step 4: Cut and place eleven 2¼" larger flower print squares on your design board. Keep moving them around until you have obtained a pleasing natural look. (Note: You may want to recut some of the squares as you gain more of an understanding of what you are trying to accomplish.) Now cut ten 2⅝" larger flower print triangles for the perimeter and put them on your design board.

Step 5: When you are satisfied with your design, sew it together using the "One-Pin, Two-Pin Sewing Method" (page 74).

Meadow Stream Design Diagram

Step 6: Enhancement. Study your quilt top and think about how it might be improved. I decided to soften the water's edge on the pattern quilt by adding a few flower patches. I used Steam-A-Seam 2 fusible webbing rather than appliqué because the additions were tiny and, frankly, the process is so much easier.

Step 7: With scissors, trim the quilt top to measure 13½" × 16½". Now you are ready to quilt and frame your piece. See page 76 for quilting suggestions and pages 64–73 for framing information.

PATTERN TWO
Lilac and Rose Bouquet by Gai Perry

Frame and Mat Size: 16" × 20"

This is the first small quilt I made and framed, so I have a sentimental attachment to it. Little bouquet quilts are fun to design, and they make a perfect decorating accent for a bedroom or bath.

Unless you can find the same floral print, it would be an exercise in futility to try to design a bouquet exactly like mine. Instead, look for a floral print with colors and flowers that you absolutely adore. Then follow the step-by-step instructions to create your own personalized arrangement.

Mixed Bouquet, Gai Perry,
Frame and Mat Size: 16" × 20"

Fabric Categories and Quantities

Flowers: ½ to ¾ of a yard of one floral print. It should have a variety of flower shapes and colors. The background of the print can be any color you choose. Here's an example of a bouquet with a light background.

Vase: ⅛ yard of a batik in a color that complements the color of the flowers. It should be either lighter or darker in value than the background fabric.

Tablecloth: ¼ yard of one print suitable for a table-cloth. It could be a little floral print like the one I used, or something entirely different; perhaps a gingham check or a paisley.

Background: ¼ yard of a fabric that is the same color as the background of your floral print. (Note: If your floral print includes empty background—that is, areas without flowers or leaves—you can cut squares from it instead of buying additional fabric for the background. *Vase of Roses and Tulips* on page 38 was created this way.)

Method

Step 1: Using the 4" template, cut one square from the floral print. It should feature two or three flowers and a few leaves. Also cut one 2¼" × 1⅜" rectangle. Place them on your design board in the positions shown in the Design Diagram. (Note: A 4" square will take up less space on the design board than four 2¼" squares.)

Step 2: Using the 2¼" template, cut some flower and leaf squares. Be flexible! Let your floral print dictate exactly where the individual flowers should be placed. (Design note: Look at the orientation of the flowers in the pattern quilt. See how they start to cascade downward toward the rim of the vase?)

Step 3: Cut two 2¼" squares, two 2⅝" triangles, and two 2⅛" triangles from the batik fabric and place them on your design board. (Design note: Try to cut the batik so that one side of the vase is a little bit lighter in value. It will give the feeling of a highlight on the vase.)

Step 4: Cut seven 2¼" squares, ten 2⅝" triangles, and two 2⅛" triangles from the tablecloth fabric and place them on your design board. I used the reverse side of some of the squares and triangles to continue the highlighted area from the vase onto the tablecloth.

Step 5: From the background fabric, cut twenty 2⅝" perimeter triangles and as many 2¼" squares and 2¼" × 1⅜" rectangles as needed to complete the design. Place them on the design board.

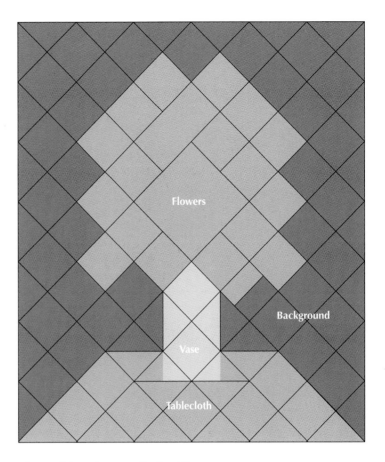

Lilac and Rose Bouquet Design Diagram

Step 6: When you are satisfied with your design, sew it together using the "One-Pin, Two-Pin Sewing Method" (page 74). (Sewing note: The triangles within the body of the quilt should be sewn into 2¼" squares before you start sewing the squares into diagonal rows.)

Step 7: Enhancement. Study your quilt top and think about how it might be improved. To make my bouquet look fuller, I added several flowers and parts of flowers using Steam-A-Seam 2 fusible webbing. Notice how I put a little patch of lilacs over the top point of the vase to soften the shape.

Step 8: With scissors, trim your quilt top to measure 13½" × 16½". Now you are ready to quilt and frame your piece. See page 76 for quilting suggestions and pages 64–73 for framing information.

PATTERN THREE

Hydrangea Bush by Gai Perry

Frame and Mat Size: 16" × 20"

When the original version of this quilt appeared in *Impressionist Palette*, I was over-whelmed by requests for the pattern. Well, here it is: a smaller interpretation perhaps, but one that's just as pleasing to the eye. If you can't find the same kind of "showy" hydrangeas, substitute another type of large flower. I used luscious red, pink, and ivory roses and the same pattern to create *Queen of Hearts Rose Bush.*

Fabric Categories and Quantities

Flowers: 1 yard of one medium or dark background floral print, or ½ yard each of two compatible floral prints. The print(s) should have single flowers that are large enough to fill a 4" square, as well as smaller flowers and attractive leaves.

Wall: ¼ yard of one textured print featuring bricks, stones, or some other architectural element. I chose a print that looked like cracked and peeling paint for *Queen of Hearts Rose Bush.*

Queen of Hearts Rose Bush, Gai Perry,
Frame and Mat Size: 16" × 20"

Method

Step 1: Using the 4" template, cut six large flower squares and place them on your design board in the spaces indicated. (Reminder: A 4" square takes up less space on the design board than four 2¼" squares.) Cut one 2¼" × 4" rectangle and place it on the design board as shown in the Hydrangea Bush Design Diagram. Be aware of the orientation of the flowers in the pattern quilt, and don't cut all the flowers pointing straight up.

Step 2: Fill in the rest of the flowering bush area with template-cut 2¼" squares of flowers and leaves. Cut sixteen 2⅝" triangles to go around the perimeter of the flowering bush area. Notice how in *Hydrangea Bush* I put brick-colored

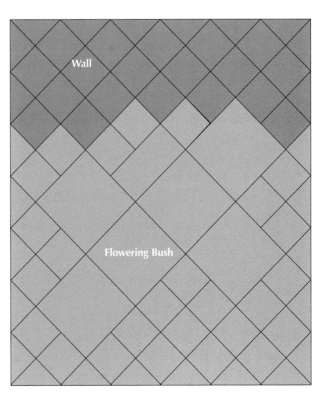

Hydrangea Bush Design Diagram

flowers next to the wall. If I had used contrasting flowers instead, I might have softened some of the square points with fusible flower patches after the quilt top was sewn.

Step 3: Cut nineteen 2¼" wall squares and ten 2⅝" wall perimeter triangles and place them on the design board. If you are using a brick print, have the east-west points of the squares touching a grout line for continuity.

Step 4: When you are satisfied with your design, sew it together using the "One-Pin, Two-Pin Sewing Method" (page 74).

Step 5: Enhancement. Study your quilt top and think about how it might be improved. In *Hydrangea Bush*, I added one purple flower and one leaf using Steam-A-Seam 2 fusible webbing. Your quilt may not need any additions, or it may need several.

Step 6: With scissors, trim your quilt top to measure 13½" × 16½". Now you are ready to quilt and frame your piece. See page 76 for quilting suggestions and pages 64–73 for framing information.

PATTERN FOUR
Field of Flowers by Gai Perry

Frame and Mat Size: 16" × 20"

This uncomplicated pattern uses just three prints, but to make it work, each one must be a realistic interpretation of sky, trees, and a flowering meadow. *Sunset* is an example of an even simpler version of this pattern. It eliminates the tree element and has a straight-line horizon.

Sunset, Gai Perry, Frame and Mat Size: 16" × 20"

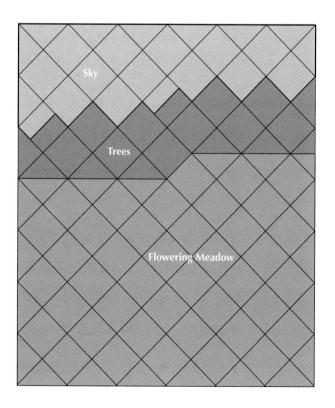

Field of Flowers Design Diagram

Fabric Categories and Quantities

Flowering Meadow: ½ yard of one floral print on a dark or medium-dark background. The flowers should look like they are growing in a meadow. It would be nice if they were graduated in size to suggest a feeling of distance. If you can't find that kind of print, purchase ¼ yard of an additional color-compatible print with slightly larger flowers for the foreground area.

Trees: ¼ yard of a realistic tree print. The shade of the leaves should match the color of the leaves on the floral print(s).

Sky: ¼ yard of an attractive print that you feel resembles sky.

Method

Step 1: Hand-cut or strip-cut forty-one 2¼" squares from the flowering meadow print, and place them on the design board. Put the larger-size flowers in the foreground, and gradually mix in the smaller flowers as you move toward the horizon line.

Step 2: When the meadow squares are in place, cut five 2⅝" meadow triangles and one 2⅛" meadow triangle for the horizon line, and put them on the design board. Then cut fourteen 2⅝" triangles for the bottom and side perimeters of the meadow. As you are cutting, think about the correct orientation of the flowers.

Step 3: Cut ten 2¼" squares from the tree print and place them on the design board. Cut and place two 2¼" × 1⅜" tree print rectangles on the design board. Cut seven 2⅝" triangles and one 2⅛" triangle from the tree print, and place them on the horizon line and the perimeter.

Step 4: Cut thirteen 2¼" squares and two 2¼" × 1⅜" rectangles from the sky print and place them on the design board. Also cut and place nine 2⅝" triangles for the perimeter of the sky.

Step 5: At this point, your design isn't going to resemble mine because of all the enhancements I added with paint and fusible webbing. Sew your quilt top together using the "One-Pin, Two-Pin Sewing Method" (page 74), and then go on to step 6.

Step 6: Enhancement. Compare your quilt top to *Field of Flowers* to see the possibilities for enhancement. To create a more natural skyline, I added several patches of the tree print with Steam-A-Seam 2 fusible webbing. I also added a patch of the meadow print to give a gentle slope to the horizon line. To create the impression of trees casting shadows on the meadow, I used green acrylic paint (you could use any green fabric paint you have on hand). First, I put a dab of paint in a small, shallow container and thinned it with water until it looked like green-tinted water. I dipped a soft artist's brush in clear water and dampened the area of the meadow near the horizon line. Then I painted over the dampened area with the watered-down green paint. When it was dry, I pressed with a hot iron to set the paint. Adding shadows this way is a nice touch, but if you feel timid about painting, don't do it.

Step 7: With scissors, trim your quilt top to measure 13½" × 16½". Now you are ready to quilt and frame your piece. See page 76 for quilting suggestions and pages 64–73 for framing information.

PATTERN FIVE

Island Inlet by Gai Perry

Frame Size: 20" × 24"

Here is a more challenging pattern for you to try. It is a smaller version of a quilt I made after my house was flooded during a winter storm. It projects a somewhat dark and moody atmosphere—a reflection of my frame of mind as the floors and walls were being repaired. I would suggest you make one of the other four Impressionist patterns first, to get your "feet wet."

Fabric Categories and Quantities

Water: ¾ yard of one water print. It should express movement and have light- and dark-value areas to create an impression of reflected light. Consider using a batik.

Sky: ½ yard of one sky print. It should be in the same color family as the water print, and ideally, it should have some lighter- and darker-value areas.

Foreground Foliage: 1 yard of a print depicting grasses and plants that might grow near a beach. The color should blend with the color of the water print.

Background Foliage: ¼ yard of a textured print that projects the color and feeling of the foreground foliage seen from a distance. Study the pattern quilt for ideas.

Treetops: ¼ yard of one realistic-looking leaf print.

Tree Trunks: ¼ yard of a brown textured print. (Note: The tree trunks will be applied with Steam-A-Seam 2 fusible webbing after the quilt is sewn.)

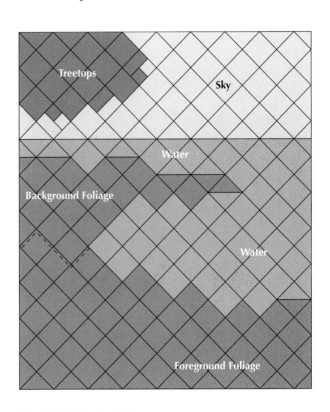

Island Inlet Design Diagram

Method

Step 1: Cut thirty-nine 2¼" squares from the water print and position them on your design board. Pay attention to the arrangement of light- and dark-value areas as shown on the pattern quilt. Cut and position eight 2⅝" water triangles along the horizon line. Also cut one 2⅛" horizon line triangle. (It appears on the far right.) Cut four 2⅝" triangles for the right perimeter of the water. Cut one 2⅛" triangle for the left perimeter of the water. Also cut six 2⅝" water triangles and place them along the inlet (as shown in the Design Diagram).

Step 2: For the foliage, start in the foreground and, depending on the scale of your foliage prints, use templates to cut various size squares. I used one 5¾" square and a couple of 4" squares, and I filled in the rest of the allotted space with 2¼" squares. You will notice that I added a couple of rock squares because their color was so perfect. Use your discretion as to the square sizes. When all the foreground foliage squares are in place, add fourteen 2⅝" perimeter triangles. Use the 2⅛" template pattern for the lower right-hand corner triangle.

Step 3: Cut fifteen 2¼" squares, seven 2⅝" triangles, and one 2⅛" triangle from the background foliage print and put them on your design board. Refer to the Design Diagram for placement.

Step 4: Cut twenty-six 2¼" squares, two 1⅜" squares, and two 2¼" × 1⅜" rectangles from the sky print and position them on your design board. Add eight 2⅝" triangles and one 2⅛" triangle, also from the sky print, to form the horizon line. Cut eight 2⅝" triangles for the sky perimeter. Cut one 2⅛" triangle for the top right corner.

Step 5: Cut eleven 2¼" squares, two 1⅜" squares, and two 1⅜" × 2¼" rectangles from the leafy print. Position them on your design board for the treetops. Then cut and add five 2⅝" perimeter triangles.

Step 6: When you are satisfied with your design, sew it together using the "One-Pin, Two-Pin Sewing Method" (page 74). (Sew smaller squares and rectangles into 2¼" squares before stitching diagonal rows.)

Step 7: Cut out two tree trunks (page 77) from the brown textured print. Attach the trunks to the quilt top with Steam-A-Seam 2 fusible webbing.

Step 8: Enhancement. Study your quilt top and think about how it might be improved. The only enhancement I thought my quilt needed was a more graceful outline of the treetops against the sky. I cut several small patches of the leafy print and used Steam-A-Seam 2 fusible webbing to attach them to the quilt top. You might want to use a paint wash, as described in Pattern Four, step 6 (page 29), to soften and blend the water into the foliage.

Step 9: Now you are ready to quilt and frame your piece. See page 76 for quilting suggestions and pages 64–73 for framing information.

GALLERY OF FRAMED QUILTS

*W*hen you begin shopping for frames, you will find a wide range of styles available. When I was selecting frames for my quilts, I seemed to gravitate toward gallery-style frames with gilt finishes for many of the Impressionist quilts and simpler strip-style frames for the traditional and contemporary pieces.

Several of the gallery quilts are designed to look like close-up photos, or isolated areas of larger quilts and landscape scenes. So, in a manner of speaking, they are not small quilts (which would imply a completed image), but rather, cropped sections from larger pieces. This "zoom lens" approach is an effective way to create drama in a small format. The quilt shown below is a good example of what I'm talking about.

Butterfly Creek, Gai Perry, Frame and Mat Size: 20" × 16"
This quilt picture invites an intimate look at a small section of water and the surrounding flowers. It gives a very subtle impression of stained glass. I think the butterflies add a nice touch of whimsy. The frame is a ready-made gallery style with an antique gilt finish.

Cottage in the Woods, Gai Perry, Frame and Mat Size: 16" × 20"
To me, this quilt seems almost too cute, but everyone I've shown it to loves it. I used just
one scenic print, but it required a whole yard to get the repeats I needed to redesign the
scene. I painted over some of the flower areas to lighten them. I think the bright gold finish
on the ready-made gallery-style frame complements the intense color scheme of the quilt.

▶

Wildflowers, Gai Perry, Frame and Mat Size: 11" × 14" Here is another one of those "zoom lens" close-up pictures I was talking about. Just a few meadow flowers and a dragonfly, but I find the colors and artistic rendering of the flowers very satisfying. The pale cream and green double mat and the silver-and-gold frame complete this Impressionist-style picture.

◀

The Bridge, Gai Perry, Frame and Mat Size: 16" × 20" I used a brick print for the bridge, but the rest of the quilt was made from one scenic print. I enjoy the challenge of cutting up this kind of print to create an entirely different picture. The deep cream mat treatment and the simple, ready-made gilt frame are a nice finishing touch.

Meadow's Edge, Gai Perry, Frame and Mat Size: 16" × 20"
I am always happy when I am working with the analogous colors of green and
blue. Color theorists suggest these hues instill a feeling of serenity and peace-
fulness. I think they are right. To complete the serene feeling, I chose a blue
and pale gray mat combination and a thin silver ready-made frame.

▲

Dragonfly Creek, Gai Perry,
Frame and Mat Size: 20" × 16"
This quilt was made from the same
pattern as the quilt on page 33, just
with a different choice of fabrics and
"critters." I love the ribbed gilt gallery-
style frame. I found it ready-made at
an art supply store.

▶

Sunlight, Gai Perry,
Frame and Mat Size: 16" × 20"
Another water scene with flowers along
the bank. The high-contrast print I used
for the water gives me the impression
of splashes of sunlight in an otherwise
shady landscape. A simple double-layer
cream mat and a silver ready-made
frame complete the picture.

Vase of Roses and Tulips, Gai Perry, Frame and Mat Size: 16" × 20"
A yellow background floral print was used to design this bouquet, and there was enough open space on the print to allow me to use it for the background of my quilt. This was a good thing, because the yellow color would have been difficult to match. I found the perfect shade of green over cream for the double-mat treatment. The ready-made frame has a mellow gold finish.

Another Island Inlet, Gai Perry, Frame Size: 20" × 24"
I wanted to show a different way to approach Pattern Five (page 30). So many of my students were locked into the idea of using foliage exclusively and were frustrated when they couldn't find the perfect kinds of plants and beach grasses. After I made this quilt, they were able to see other possibilities. Silver-finish metal framing strips complete the picture.

Forest in Winter, Gai Perry, Frame and Mat Size: 16" × 20"

Icy gray-blue water, barren trees, and frosty-looking wild grass; it couldn't be any other season but winter. This forest scene was created with just two prints. I think the blue and pale gray mat combination together with the silver ready-made frame emphasizes the coolness of the scene.

Forest in Fall, Gai Perry, Frame and Mat Size: 16" × 20"
Same forest pattern, different season. I enhanced the scene by adding several more small
blue flowers with fusible webbing. Three fabrics were used to make this quilt picture. When
I found the ready-made carved wood frame, I knew it would look terrific on this fall scene.

◄

Hollyhocks, Gai Perry,
Frame and Mat Size:
14" × 11"
All I did here was cut
squares and triangles
from one floral fabric
and arrange them to
look like a bed of holly-
hocks. I added stalks
from the same print
(with fusible webbing)
to make the flowers
look thicker and more
colorful. The scene is so
simple that I think the
ornate ready-made
gallery frame provides
a nice contrast.

Love Letters, Gai Perry,
Frame Size: 24" × 12"
I don't know why I made this quilt. Maybe because I
wanted to try some letter piecing, or maybe I was looking
forward to Valentine's Day. My granddaughters were visit-
ing me while I was putting it together and they liked it, so
now it hangs in their bedroom. The quilt is made with 1"
(finished size) squares and triangles. I had the frame
custom-made, but I did the mounting.

Evening Stars, Gai Perry, Frame Size: 18" × 22"

This little quilt was the focus of one of my early color lessons. The challenge was to create a design that incorporated a variety of fabrics: plaids, stripes, checks, polka dots, florals, and solids; large-, medium-, and small-scale prints; and light, medium, and dark values. The purpose was to encourage students to put a wider variety of print styles in their quilts. The Evening Star block measures 5" after sewing. I had the metal frame custom-made because I couldn't resist the pink color.

Mirror Image, Gai Perry, Frame Size: 18" × 27"
Designing this quilt was so much fun, I finally had to tell myself to stop playing and sew it.
The 4½" (finished size) block is made with two 5³⁄₈" half-square triangles. One triangle has
three 1½" strips running horizontally, the other has six 1½" strips running vertically. All
kinds of mirror images are possible as long as you make a duplicate of each block for the
mirror-imaging effect. To finish this quilt, I used black metal framing strips.

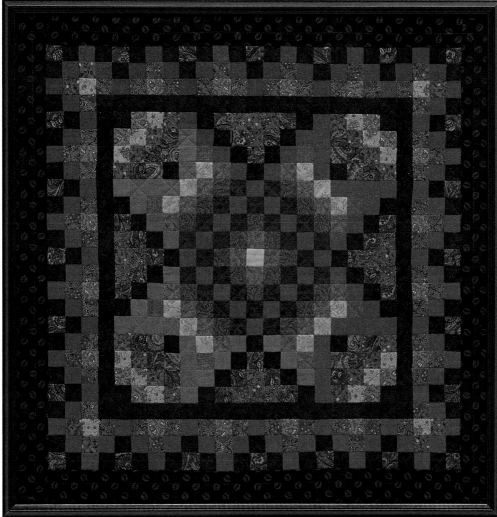

Geometric Star, Gai Perry, Frame Size: 28" × 28" One of my own larger quilts, shown at right, inspired this star design. The framed version is made with 1" (finished size) squares. Wood framing strips were used to complete the picture.

The Jewel Tree, Gai Perry, Frame and Mat Size: 11" × 14"
I love pictorial quilt blocks and trees are a particular favorite. I think one
sparkling tree can stand by itself very nicely. The piece was finished with
a black and white mat combination and black metal framing strips.

▲

Night Wings, Gai Perry,
Frame Size: 25" × 25"
Here is the same little 3" block I
used for Pattern Six (page 52), but
what a difference the choice of
fabrics and setting makes. Black
metal framing strips, like those I
used on this quilt, are a good
choice for framing square quilts.

▶

Game Board, Gai Perry,
Frame Size: 21" × 21"
I have a scrap file filled with
primitive game board photos that
I've cut from country decorating
magazines. Game board designs
translated into fabric make won-
derfully graphic wallhangings.
Black metal framing strips are
just the right finishing touch for
this quilt.

Checkerboard One-Patch, Gai Perry, Frame and Mat Size: 16" × 20"
This is the simplest of all quilt designs, but the colorful squares juxtaposed with the
black and white print (and the kelly green mat) make a bold statement. A black
metal ready-made frame was the obvious choice to complete the color scheme.

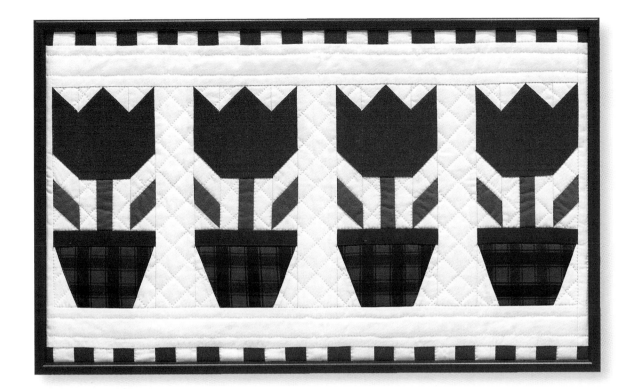

▲

Christmas Tulips, Gai Perry,
Frame Size: 28" × 17"
I made this quilt years ago
and can't even remember if
the block was original or one
I copied. When I started writing *Do-It-Yourself Framed
Quilts*, I decided to put a
custom-made cherry red
frame around it. What a
difference a frame makes!

▶

Paul's Apple Basket, Gai Perry,
Frame Size: 15" × 15"
When I was first learning how
to quilt, I took a six-week class
from Paul Pilgrim. Each week
he would present an original
basket design, and we were
to re-create it using our own
ideas for the colors and fabrics. This block had so many
itsy-bitsy pieces, the idea of
making more than one was
overwhelming. I put a border
on it and stored it with all my
other never-to-be-seen-again
quilts. The white metal frame
was custom-made, but I
mounted the quilt to
keep the cost down.

Vintage Crazy, maker unknown,
Frame and Mat Size: 18" × 27"
This is a segment from an old crazy quilt that I found in an
antique shop. It was already matted and framed. Lucky me!

TRADITIONAL AND CONTEMPORARY QUILTS

*H*ave you ever wondered what makes a traditional quilt different from a contemporary quilt? Maybe these dictionary definitions will help.

**traditional—handed down by, or conforming to, an established pattern
contemporary—of or in the style of the present or recent times**

The conclusion I draw is that if you work exclusively with historical patterns and make an effort to use only fabrics that appear to have an age factor of at least fifty years, then you are a traditional quilter. On the other hand, if you work with fabrics that have a distinct "now" look and enjoy putting your own spin on traditional blocks or inventing new ones, then you're a contemporary quilter.

I'm an enthusiastic fan of both styles, and I like to move back and forth between the two. I get a kick out of using wildly contemporary fabrics to interpret a traditional block (see *Things That Go 'Round* on page 58), but there are some design instances where I draw the line. I'm a fanatic about not putting traditional and contemporary fabrics into the same quilt. No way! Can't do it! I wouldn't dream of putting a gingham check or a cutesy floral into a contemporary quilt . . . or a batik in a traditional piece (see *Nineteenth Century Revisited* on the following page). I'm a firm believer that the impact and authenticity of a quilt can be diluted when fabrics from different time periods are commingled.

The point of view I have just expressed is one of my particular idiosyncrasies, but it doesn't have to be one of yours. In this modern age of quilting, anything goes. All the dos and don'ts have been thrown out the window, leaving a nice airy space for creativity to flourish.

You will find both traditional and contemporary quilt styles represented in this pattern section; how you re-create them is entirely your choice. The instructions assume that you have basic piecing skills. If you have trouble piecing the patterns, take a beginners' class or consult one of the excellent how-to books listed under Reference Books (page 79).

PATTERN SIX

Nineteenth Century Revisited by Gai Perry

Frame Size: 20" × 23"

As far as I know, this little quilt block is nameless, but it is very versatile and can assume many identities. The pattern quilt contains a collection of reproduction nineteenth-century prints. If this antique look appeals to you, test your knowledge of period-style prints by re-creating your own version of this vintage-looking quilt.

If you are more interested in a contemporary look, take a look at *Night Wings* (page 47). This interpretation uses the exact same 3" block, just a different set.

Fabric Categories and Quantities

Lots of scraps! Assemble a good assortment of lighter- and darker-value prints. They shouldn't be too light or too dark. The idea is for the quilt to look mellow and somewhat aged. I must have used at least forty different pink, tan, brown, and cream prints in my version of the pattern. I purchased eighth-yard cuts of twelve different fabrics and pulled the rest from my stash. The more fabrics you use, the more antique-looking the finished quilt will be.

You will also need ⅓ yard of a lighter-value print for the "edging strips."

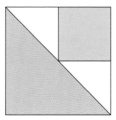

3" Quilt Block

Method

The block is made with one large darker-value triangle, two small lighter-value triangles, and one darker-value square. The cutting directions may sound vague, but that is the nature of scrap quilts.

Step 1: To start the design process, cut two 3⅞" squares and three 2" squares from each of the darker-value prints. Cut each of the 3⅞" squares diagonally from corner to corner to create the larger triangles.

Step 2: Cut three 3⅜" squares from each of the lighter-value prints. Cut these squares diagonally from corner to corner in both directions to create the smaller triangles.

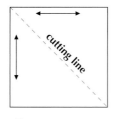 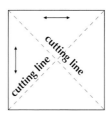

3⅞" square   3⅜" square

Step 3: Steps 1 and 2 will give you enough cut pieces to start the design. Begin arranging the squares and triangles on your design board, referring to the Quilt Diagram for placement. When you run out, cut some more.

Nineteenth
Century Revisited
Quilt Diagram

Step 4: When you are satisfied with your design, sew the individual blocks together. First stitch the two smaller triangles to the square; press both seam allowances toward the square. Then join the larger triangle, pressing toward the larger triangle. Sew the completed blocks into rows and then sew the rows together. Press.

Step 5: Cut four 3" strips from the "edging strip" print to the appropriate lengths and stitch them to the four sides of the quilt top, as if you were adding a border. Press. Later on, these strips can be trimmed down to allow more flexibility when determining the frame size.

Step 6: Now you are ready to quilt and frame your piece. See page 76 for quilting suggestions and pages 64–73 for framing information.

PATTERN SEVEN
Concentric Diamonds by Gai Perry

Frame Size: 26" × 30"

This quilt excites me! I love the hard-edged contemporary look and the fact that even though it's small, it can be seen and appreciated from a distance. I used cobalt blue and acid green textured prints, but if I had worked with the collection of fabrics I used in *Nineteenth Century Revisited* (page 52), the ultimate effect would have been softer-looking and more traditional.

Fabric Categories and Quantities

Concentric Diamonds was designed with scraps of medium-dark to dark blue prints, and light to medium-light green prints. Use as many as you can get your hands on. Look for tone-on-tone and subtly patterned prints that, when sewn, suggest a feeling of textured cloth, rather than individual triangles. You will also need ⅜ yard of a dark blue textured print for the "edging strips."

Concentric Diamonds Design Diagram (Notice the changing direction of the pairs of triangles.)

Method

Step 1: Cut! Cut! Cut! Cut several 2⅞" squares from each of the dark and medium-dark prints. Cut each square diagonally from corner to corner to make two triangles. Cut several 4⅛" squares from each of the light and medium-light prints. Cut each of these squares diagonally in both directions to form four triangles. When triangles are cut in this manner, there is less tendency for them to stretch during sewing. (Note: You will probably have to cut more as the design grows.)

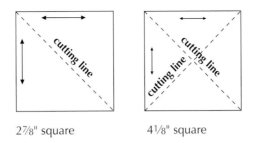

2⅞" square   4⅛" square

Step 2: Starting in the center of the quilt, begin putting the triangles on your design board. Refer to the Design Diagram for placement. Design suggestions: Notice how the medium-dark blue prints are mixed with a few dark blue prints to create the inner rectangle. The darkest blue prints are used exclusively to define the outer rectangle. The light and medium-light greens commingle to create a sparkle effect.

Step 3: When the design is completed to your satisfaction, start sewing. Begin by sewing all the opposing triangles into squares. Press toward the darker triangles and clip all the little tails. Put all the newly formed squares back on the design board in the correct position. Starting with the bottom row, use the "One-Pin, Two-Pin Sewing Method" (page 74) to sew squares together in rows. Press the seam allowances for each row in one direction only and alternate the direction from row to row. Stitch the rows together and press all the seam allowances in the same direction, either up or down.

Setup for the "One-Pin, Two-Pin Sewing Method" for Joining Squares. (Turn to pages 74–75 for additional information about this sewing method.)

Step 4: Cut four 3" strips from the "edging strip" print to the appropriate lengths and stitch them to the four sides of the quilt top. Press. Later they will allow more flexibility in determining the frame size.

Step 5: Now you are ready to quilt and frame your piece. See page 76 for quilting suggestions and pages 64–73 for framing information.

PATTERN EIGHT

Things That Go 'Round by Gai Perry

Frame Size: 22" × 22"

This pattern is a variation of a traditional pinwheel block. The obvious way to handle it would be to alternate light- and dark-value prints, but I decided to have a little fun. I chose a group of contemporary prints that would exaggerate the movement of the pinwheels, and I substituted bright prints for the light ones. This pattern would also be marvelous in just two alternating fabrics, one colorful print plus white or black.

Fabric Categories and Quantities

Fabric One: ⅓ yard of a warm, bright focus print

Fabric Two: ¼ yard of a cool, dark focus print

Fabric Three: ¼ yard of a stripe featuring the warm, bright color

Fabric Four: ¼ yard of a stripe featuring the cool, dark color

Fabric Five: ⅛ yard of a warm, bright solid accent color

Fabric Six: ⅛ yard of a cool, dark accent print or solid

Fabric Seven: ⅛ yard of a check print featuring the cool, dark color

Fabric Eight: ½ yard of a warm, bright print or solid for the "edging strips." (Design note: Fabrics Five and Eight can be the same or different.)

10" Pinwheel Block (Numbers indicate placement of fabrics one through seven.)

Method

Step 1: Use the pinwheel template patterns (page 78) to cut the following quantities of each fabric: 16 of Fabric One, 12 of Fabric Two, 16 of Fabric Three, 16 of Fabric Four, 16 of Fabric Five, 16 of Fabric Six, and 4 of Fabric Seven. Observe the grainline arrows when cutting Fabric Three and Fabric Four so the stripes run in the right direction. Arrange the pattern pieces on your design board in the correct order, and critique. If you like what you see, go on to Step 2.

Step 2: Sew 16 A units, 12 B units, and 4 C units. Press seam allowances toward the darker print.

Unit A   (Make 16)   Unit B   (Make 12)   Unit C   (Make 4)

Step 3: Sew A units to B units to make 12 D units. Sew remaining A units to C units to make 4 E units.

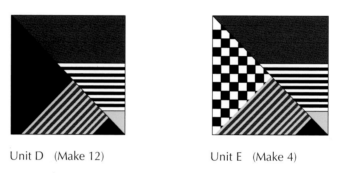

Unit D   (Make 12)   Unit E   (Make 4)

Step 4: Sew 3 D units and 1 E unit into a pinwheel block. Press. Repeat three times.

Step 5: Referring to the pattern quilt, arrange the four blocks and sew them together. Press.

Step 6: Cut four 3" strips of Fabric Eight to the appropriate lengths and stitch them to the four sides of the quilt top, as if you were adding a border. These are "edging strips." Later on, these strips can be trimmed down to allow more flexibility when determining the frame size.

10" Pinwheel Block

Step 7: Now you are ready to quilt and frame your piece. See page 76 for quilting suggestions and pages 64–73 for framing information.

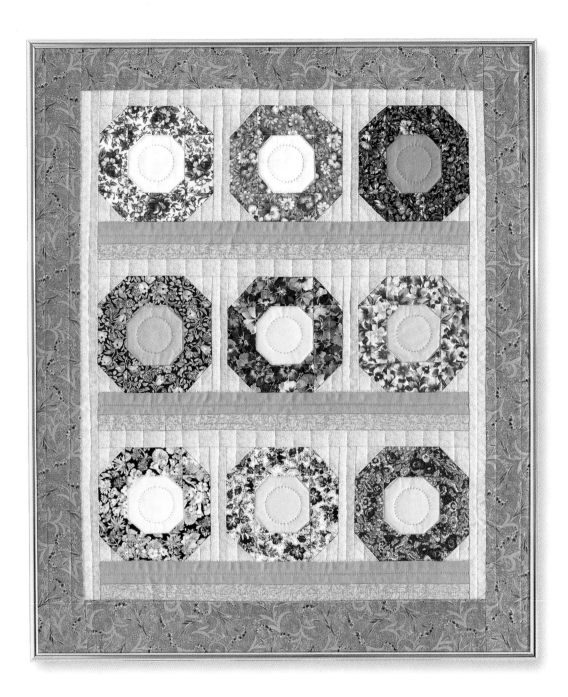

PATTERN NINE

Chintzware Plates by Gai Perry

Frame Size: 22" × 26"

Chintzware is a style of china tableware mass-produced in the early twentieth century. It has become extremely collectible in recent years. I think much of its popularity is due to the extensive articles and publicity given to it by *Victoria* magazine. In any case, the diverse and charming floral patterns found on this vintage china inspired *Chintzware Plates*.

Fabric Categories and Quantities

Plate Rims: ⅛ yard each of nine floral prints

Plate Centers: Scraps of nine different solid-color fabrics

Background: ½ yard of a small-scale print

Plate Shelves: ¼ yard of print A and ¼ yard of print B

Edging Border: ½ yard of a print suitable for the "edging strips"

Method

Step 1: Design nine 5" plate blocks. For each plate block, cut one Plate Center (A) using the template (page 63). From each of the floral prints, cut the follow-

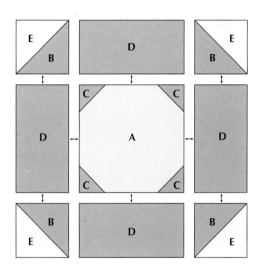

Construction of 5" Plate Block

ing: two 2⅛" squares, then cut each in half diagonally to form four triangles (B); two 1½" squares, then cut each in half diagonally to form four triangles (C); and four 3" × 1¾" rectangles (D). From the background print, cut two 2⅛" squares, then cut each in half diagonally to form four triangles (E). Position the pieces for all nine plates on your design board and critique. If you like the fabrics you have chosen, sew the nine plate blocks. If not, substitute other fabrics.

Step 2: Cut six 1¼" × 5½" strips from the background print. Sew three plate blocks and two strips together for each of the three rows.

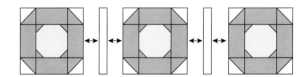

Step 3: To make the plate shelves, cut three 1½" × 17" strips from print A and three 1¼" × 17" strips from print B. Sew each A strip to a B strip along the length of the strip. Press. Attach one shelf unit to the lower edge of each plate row.

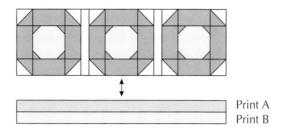

Print A
Print B

Step 4: Cut three 1¼" × 17" strips from the background print and attach one to the top edge of each row of plates. Press. Sew the three units together. Press.

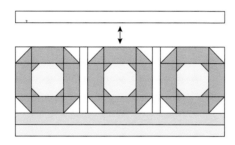

Step 5: Measure the length of your quilt top. From the background fabric, cut two 1¼" strips to that length. Attach them to the left and right sides of your quilt. Press.

Step 6: Cut four 4"-wide strips from the "edging" print to the appropriate lengths and stitch them to the four sides of your quilt top. Press.

Step 7: Now you are ready to quilt and frame your piece. See page 76 for quilting suggestions and pages 64–73 for framing information.

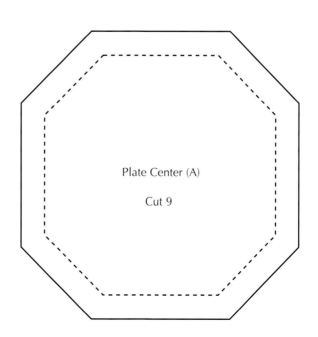

Plate Center (A)

Cut 9

FRAMING

*O*nce I had designed and made my first few quilt pictures, I went to the library thinking I would pick up some useful books about ready-made framing. To my disappointment, there weren't any. The only books I found were dedicated to making frames from scratch using a miter box and a room full of tools. This was something I definitely didn't want to do, so I started compiling my own framing portfolio, including information about what kinds of ready-made frames were available and where to buy them.

The primary focus of my research was keeping the cost of framing as low as possible. And here are three very good reasons.

- **So quilters can give the finished pieces to friends and family.**
- **So quilters can see higher profits when their pieces are sold at quilt shows and fund-raisers.**
- **So quilters can decorate their homes without taking out a bank loan.**

After a bit of trial and error, and with the help of a professional framer who very kindly walked me through the whole process, I discovered that do-it-yourself framing is easy. And this may sound naive, but I found that framing one of my quilts and turning it into artwork to hang on the wall was profoundly satisfying.

Ready-Made Frames

A frame should enhance the image it surrounds, not compete for attention. This is particularly true when it comes to framing a quilt. Because there is so much action on the surface of a quilt—the design, colors, fabric patterns, quilting stitches—I find simple frames are best.

Ready-made frames are available in a range of sizes. Some styles even come packaged with glass and hanging devices. If you select a wooden gallery-style frame that doesn't include glass, the store will usually have the right size glass in stock or can cut it for a small additional price.

POPULAR READY-MADE FRAME SIZES

8" × 10"	18" × 24"
9" × 12"	20" × 24"
11" × 14"	22" × 28"
12" × 16"	24" × 30"
16" × 20"	24" × 36"

Ready-Made Framing Strips

Of all the frame styles shown in the Gallery (pages 33–50), my personal favorite is a metal strip-style frame in a finish that complements the individual quilt. These metal framing strips come two to a package in lengths ranging from 6" to 40" in 1" increments. You have to buy one package for the length and another for the width to create your desired frame size.

Metal framing strips are sold at most art and craft stores. The price is reasonable, and everything you need to assemble the frame (except a screwdriver) is included. The surface finishes include silver, pewter, black, copper, and gold. You can also find precut wood framing strips in a nice walnut or oak finish that are easy to assemble, too. I like framing strips because they allow me to create frames for quilts that don't conform to the popular ready-made frame dimensions.

Precut Mats

If the quilt you plan to frame measures less than 16" × 20", a mat will make it look more important. Mats come in all sorts of delicious colors and are available in single or double layers. I prefer double-layer mats because they add an extra dimension of color, much like an inner and outer border on a quilt.

A double-layer mat also keeps the glass from touching your quilt, a feature my framing expert says is very important. A framed quilt must have some breathing space. If you use a single-layer mat, you will have to attach clear plastic spacing strips under the glass to raise it up off the quilt surface. Avoid this step because the strips are expensive. In other words, don't purchase single-layer mats! I learned the hard way.

Make sure the package labeling indicates that the mat is acid-free. An acid-free mat is free of chemicals that could eventually stain or yellow the fabrics in your quilt. When selecting a mat, make sure the opening is at least one inch smaller in length and width than the measurement of your quilt. This will keep your quilt from migrating.

POPULAR PRECUT MAT SIZES

Overall Dimensions	Mat Opening
8" × 10"	4½" × 6½"
9" × 12"	5½" × 8½"
11" × 14"	7½" × 9½"
12" × 16"	8½" × 11½"
16" × 20"	10½" × 13½"

When to Use Glass

If you plan to mat your quilt picture, glass is advisable to keep the mat surface in pristine condition. If you plan to frame your quilt without using a mat, glass isn't necessary. Three types of framing glass are available: regular glass, nonreflective glass, and archival glass. Regular glass throws off some reflection, but I still prefer it to nonreflective glass, which dulls the color of the image it is covering. Archival glass is clear and nonreflective, but extremely expensive.

Frame and Mat Sources

Craft Stores. Large craft retailers (particularly a chain like Michaels®) are terrific sources for precut mats, ready-made frames, and framing strips. They generally offer a wide range of styles and frequently have sales giving thirty to fifty percent off.

Art Supply Stores. Art supply stores offer a good assortment of packaged frames, as well as fancier gallery-style frames, but I have found that the prices can be a little higher than at craft stores. Acid-free mats can be more expensive here, too.

Framing Stores. Stores specializing in ready-made frames and precut mats seem to be popping up all over. They have tons of frames and mats to choose from, but shop carefully because prices are sometimes higher than those at craft or art supply stores.

Antique Shops, Tag Sales, Thrift Stores, and Flea Markets. I used to find wonderful old frames at bargain prices, but apparently those days are long gone, at least in California. Maybe you'll have better luck in your part of the country. Recently, I spent a whole day wandering through some local antique and thrift shops. The few frames I found were in poor condition and outrageously overpriced. The day wasn't totally wasted, however, because in one of the shops I found the antique crazy quilt segment shown on page 50. It was hanging near the ceiling and the proprietor had to climb a ladder to get it for me. Miraculously, it was already framed, and the bright red mat and gilt frame were in perfect condition. The asking price was so low, I thought I'd died and gone to heaven. This is why I love to shop in these kinds of stores. I never know what kind of treasure I'll find.

Custom Framing

Occasionally I splurge and order custom mats and/or frames. Yes, I have to spend more money, but I justify the cost by telling myself that for these particular quilts, this was the best solution. My reasons are usually that I want a special color mat, a particular frame, or an unusual size that isn't available any other way. But even with custom framing, you can save the labor charges if you order the mat and frame and then do the mounting yourself.

The Framing Process

You have finished your quilt and are ready to frame it. First, you must decide whether you want to mat your quilt picture. If the answer is yes, go about choosing a mat the same way you would choose a border. The color should complement the quilt, not overpower it. Sometimes a colored mat makes too strong a statement. In that case, use a cream mat with a black undermat. This combination will make your quilt look very painterly and professional. I always take my quilt with me when I audition mats and frames in order to get a good idea of what the finished picture will look like.

YOUR EQUIPMENT

How you choose to frame your quilt will determine what items you need. Please don't feel overwhelmed by the number of items listed. The framing process is really very easy. Trust me!

- Frame or framing strips (make sure the back rim is deep enough to hold the mat, glass, and backing)
- Precut acid-free double-layered mat
- Acid-free tape or white linen tape (available at framing and art supply stores)
- Glass (if you mat your quilt)
- Brown acid-free kraft paper and white glue (for wood frames only)
- Sequin pins
- Acid-free foam-core backing
- Glazing points (for wood framing strips only; available at framing and hardware stores)
- Screw eyes
- Picture wire
- Flathead screwdriver
- Putty knife (for pushing in the glazing points)
- Awl (for making starter holes in the back of the frame for the screw eyes)

HOW TO MAT AND FRAME A QUILT

I have found there are several "right" ways to frame a quilt. Some of the methods I have devised are different from those used by professional framers. For instance, a professional framer will usually drill a series of holes around the perimeter of the foam-core backing and actually stitch the quilt to it. I have come up with an easier, less permanent method that uses either acid-free tape or tiny sequin pins. I like these methods because a quilt can easily be removed from the frame and replaced with another one. Sort of like having a revolving quilt show in your home.

Step 1: Select an appropriate mat and frame. If the frame doesn't come with glass, ask a salesperson to cut a piece for you. Also have an acid-free foam-core backing cut to the same size as the glass. It will replace the cardboard backing that may have been packaged with the frame. The cost is minimal, but more important, your backing

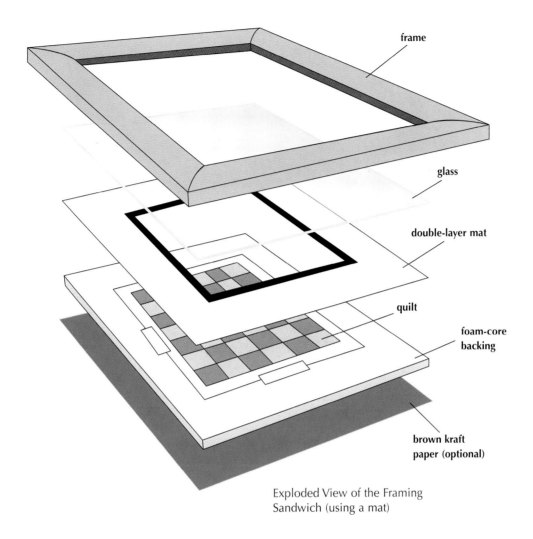

frame

glass

double-layer mat

quilt

foam-core backing

brown kraft paper (optional)

Exploded View of the Framing Sandwich (using a mat)

will be free of harmful chemicals. Acid-free foam-core comes in two thicknesses, ³⁄₁₆" and ⅛". I prefer the thinner ⅛" size.

If you are purchasing framing strips, choose your length and width packages to match the size of the mat. You will also need to buy the corresponding size glass and an acid-free foam-core backing.

Step 2: Work on a clean, protected surface such as a cloth-covered dining table. Place the quilt face up in the center of the acid-free foam-core backing, and cover it with the mat. Now you will have to go back and forth, lifting the mat and adjusting the quilt until the part of the quilt you want to show is centered under the mat. Carefully lift the mat one more time and set it aside. Put a piece of acid-free tape at four points around the edge of the quilt to secure its position on the foam-core backing (Diagram A). Replace the mat.

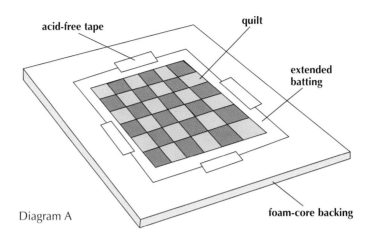

acid-free tape   quilt

extended batting

foam-core backing

Diagram A

Step 3: Clean the glass and make sure it is dry before putting it on top of the matted quilt.

Step 4: Place the frame on top of the glass, then carefully turn the framing sandwich over so the foam-core backing is facing toward you. If you are using framing strips, assemble three of the sides according to the package directions, but leave the fourth side open. Slide the matted quilt, the glass, and the foam-core backing into the frame and then attach the fourth side.

Step 5: Metal frames and framing strips come packaged with special clips. Simply snap the clips into position to hold the framing sandwich in place. If you are using a wood frame, you will need to push in several glazing points to hold the framing sandwich together. I use a putty knife or a flathead screwdriver to push the glazing points into the back edge of the frame (Diagram B).

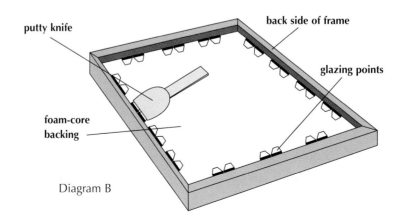

putty knife   back side of frame

glazing points

foam-core backing

Diagram B

Step 6: For wood frames only (optional): The purpose of this step is to keep dust and little critters from getting into the framing sandwich. I usually omit it, but if you are a perfectionist, read on. Squeeze a thin bead of white glue along the back edge of the frame. Spread the glue with a damp sponge. Cover the back of the frame with a piece of brown acid-free kraft paper that has been cut at least 2" larger than the frame all around. Stretch it over the back of the frame and press it against the glued surface. When the glue is dry, trim the paper to the size of the frame. If the paper looks wrinkled and "saggy," spray it with a fine mist of water and it should tighten.

Step 7: In order to hang your picture, you will need to add screw eyes and wire.

For wood frames: From top back edge, measure about a third of the way down each side of the frame and make a pencil mark. With an awl, punch in a small starter hole at each mark. Twist a screw eye into each hole. (Note: I insert the point of the awl into the screw eye to help with the twisting.)

For metal framing strips: Attach the screw eyes that are included in the package.

Step 8: Cut a piece of picture wire approximately 6" longer than the distance from eye to eye. Thread the wire into one of the screw eyes and wind the shorter end around the longer end five or six times so it won't slip. Stretch the wire across the frame and thread it into the other screw eye and wind to secure (Diagram C). Make sure the wire isn't so long that it will extend beyond the top of the frame when hanging on the wall.

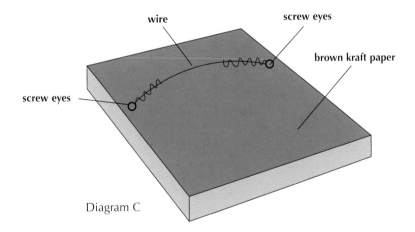

Diagram C

HOW TO FRAME A QUILT WITHOUT A MAT AND GLASS

Step 1: Measure the length and width of your quilt to determine whether you can use a ready-made frame. If your quilt doesn't conform to a ready-made frame size, the alternative is framing strips.

For ready-made frames: Purchase a frame with an opening that comes the closest to, but is not larger than, the size of your quilt. If your quilt has an edging strip or border, decide approximately how much of it you want to show and select the frame accordingly. If the frame comes with a cardboard backing, discard it and have a piece of acid-free foam-core cut to the exact size of the frame opening.

For framing strips: Purchase one package of strips for the length and another for the width. Have a piece of acid-free foam-core backing cut to the exact length and width dimensions. Example: If you are buying a 16" package and a 20" package, the foam-core backing should be 16" × 20".

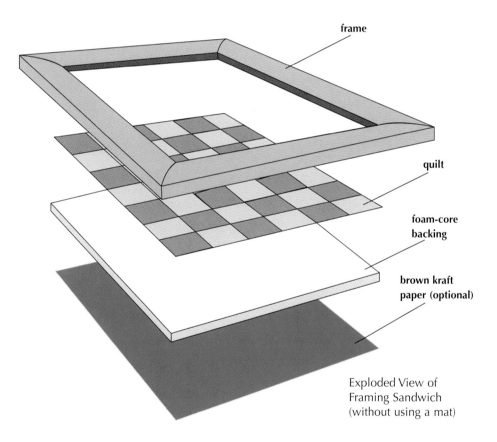

frame

quilt

foam-core backing

brown kraft paper (optional)

Exploded View of Framing Sandwich (without using a mat)

Step 2: Work on a clean, protected surface such as a cloth-covered dining table. Attach the quilt to the foam-core backing. Because frames are always perfectly in-square, and quilts rarely are, the process of attaching your quilt to a foam-core backing is an inexact science. This is how I do it.

First, with a ruler and permanent ink pen, mark the center point on each of the four edges of the foam-core backing. Now, put your quilt on top of the foam-core backing and, by eyeballing or measuring, line up the marks to correspond with the midpoints on your quilt. (Note: At this point, your quilt will probably be larger than the foam-core.)

Temporarily secure your quilt to the midpoints on the foam-core with four regular-size pins. Check to see if your quilt looks straight and if the edging strip (if used) shows evenly around the perimeter. If not, do some adjusting.

Working from the four center points to the corners, place sequin pins (they are very small) around the edge of the quilt. Push the pins in at an angle so they go through the quilt and into, but not all the way through, the foam-core. This is a little tricky. (Note: The pins will be covered by the lip of the frame.)

Finally, using sharp scissors, trim away any part of the quilt that extends over the edges of the foam-core. Don't be concerned about cutting your quilt. The Impressionist quilt patterns are designed to be slightly larger than necessary to accommodate the possibility of trimming. The traditional and contemporary quilt patterns have an added "edging strip" or a border that can easily be cut down to get an exact fit.

Step 3: When your quilt is secured to the foam-core backing, place the frame on top of the quilt and follow the same procedure as steps 4 through 8 of the previous set of instructions, but omit the glass.

Signing Your Quilt Pictures

You will probably want to attach a cloth label to the back of your quilt before framing it. It should state your name, the name of the quilt, the date the quilt was made, and where it was made. After the quilt is framed, repeat this information on the back of the framing sandwich. Doing it in your own handwriting adds a nice artistic touch.

SEWING AND QUILTING SUGGESTIONS

One-Pin, Two-Pin Sewing Method

This is a fast, accurate way to sew an Impressionist-style quilt and, amazingly, all the squares end up in the right place. You will start by sewing the squares into diagonal strips with a triangle at each end. The directions may sound confusing at first, but if you do them one step at a time, you are going to be an enthusiastic convert to this One-Pin, Two-Pin Sewing Method. It also works when you are sewing straight rows of squares together.

Step 1: Place one pin in the top triangle along the perimeter edge. Place two pins in the lower triangle along the perimeter edge.

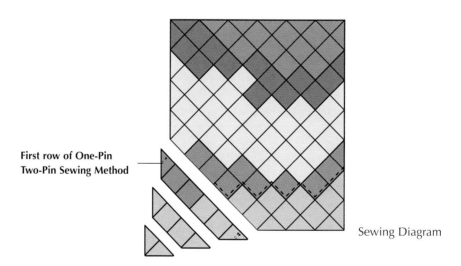

First row of One-Pin Two-Pin Sewing Method

Sewing Diagram

Step 2: Starting with the first row of the sewing method, sew the One-Pin triangle to the square sitting diagonally below it. With the presser foot still down, sew a few more stitches and leave the One-Pin Unit in the machine.

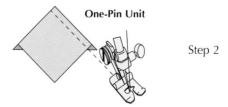

One-Pin Unit

Step 2

Step 3: From the bottom edge of the same row, sew the Two-Pin triangle to the square sitting diagonally above it. With the presser foot still down, sew a few more stitches and leave the Two-Pin Unit in the machine. With scissors, detach the One-Pin Unit.

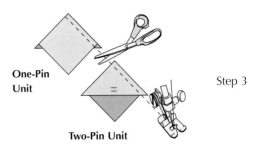

Step 3

Step 4: Move back to the top of the row and pick up the next square in sequence. Sew it to the One-Pin Unit. With the presser foot still down, sew a few more stitches and then leave this unit in the machine. With scissors, detach the Two-Pin Unit.

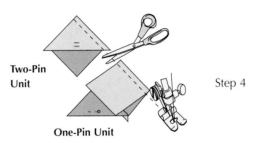

Step 4

Step 5: Move down to the lower end of the row and pick up the next square in the sequence. Sew it to the Two-Pin Unit. With the presser foot still down, sew a few more stitches and leave this unit in the machine. Detach the One-pin unit.

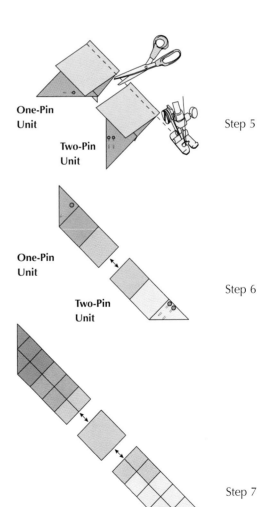

Step 5

Step 6

Step 7

Joining Large Squares

Step 6: Continue sewing in this manner until all the squares in the row are joined to the One-Pin or Two-Pin units. Sew the two units together and then pin the resulting strip onto the design board in the correct position.

Step 7: Joining and Pressing. Press the seam allowances for each row in one direction only and alternate the direction from row to row. When all the rows are sewn into strips, sew the strips together. Choose a pressing direction and press all the rows either up or down.

In rows where there are one or more large squares or rectangles, two single rows must be joined together before adding them to the larger pieces.

Quilting and Finishing

Quilting stitches do more than just bind a quilt to its backing. They capture the light and give a soft, subtle texture to an otherwise one-dimensional surface. They are also a marvelous way for you to express your individuality. In other words, do your own thing! If you are a new quilter, turn to page 79 for a list of how-to quilting books.

Choose a batting that will produce the flattest surface possible. If you have read *Color From the Heart*, you know that I quilt everything by hand. But, recently, all that has changed. I finally learned how to machine-quilt. And what a time-saver it is! Now I can say, with authority, that I like Fairfield Soft Touch® for machine quilting. For hand quilting, I still like Mountain Mist Quilt Light®.

Quilt the Impressionist designs using the diagonal grid pattern shown here or create your own quilting pattern. When I am hand-quilting, I use 100% cotton and change my thread to match the color area I'm working on. When I machine-quilt, I use a clear filament thread for the top and a light-color cotton thread for the bobbin.

Diagonal Grid Quilting Pattern

Pressing your quilt is a simple, but important, last step. After quilting, carefully press your quilt with a medium-heat, polyester setting. No hot irons, please! This blocking process makes the quilting stitches look smaller and more even.

Finishing? Don't need to! Here's the good part! The edges of the quilt are going to be covered by a mat or a frame, so you don't have to bother with a binding. You don't even have worry about whether it's in-square. Just trim the batting and backing to approximately 1" beyond the edge of the quilt top on all four sides and you're done. Your quilt is ready for framing. (Note: If you're framing a previously finished quilt, it's not necessary to cut off the binding.)

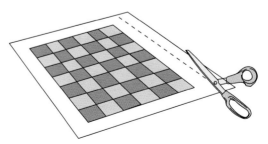

Trim the four sides to approximately 1" beyond the quilt top.

Template Patterns

Impressionist Quilts

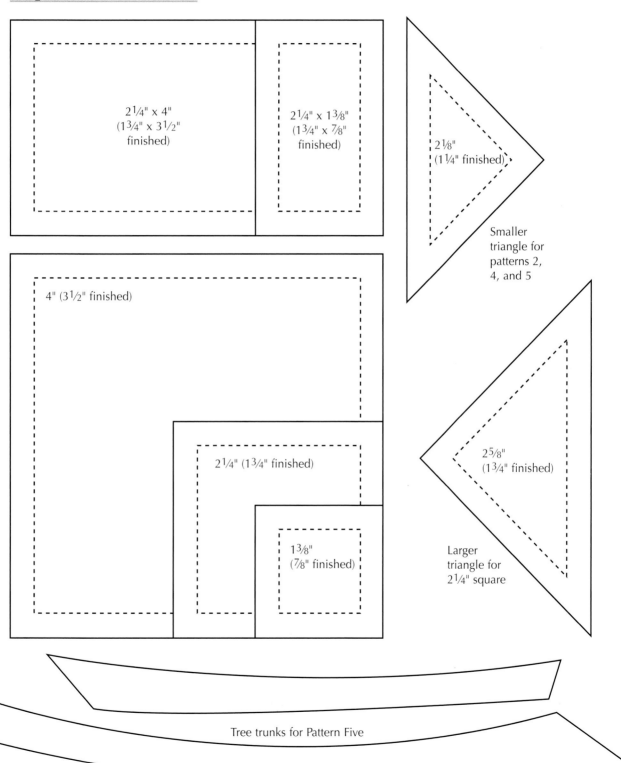

2¼" x 4"
(1¾" x 3½"
finished)

2¼" x 1⅜"
(1¾" x ⅞"
finished)

2⅛"
(1¼" finished)

Smaller
triangle for
patterns 2,
4, and 5

4" (3½" finished)

2¼" (1¾" finished)

2⅝"
(1¾" finished)

1⅜"
(⅞" finished)

Larger
triangle for
2¼" square

Tree trunks for Pattern Five

Things That Go 'Round Template Patterns

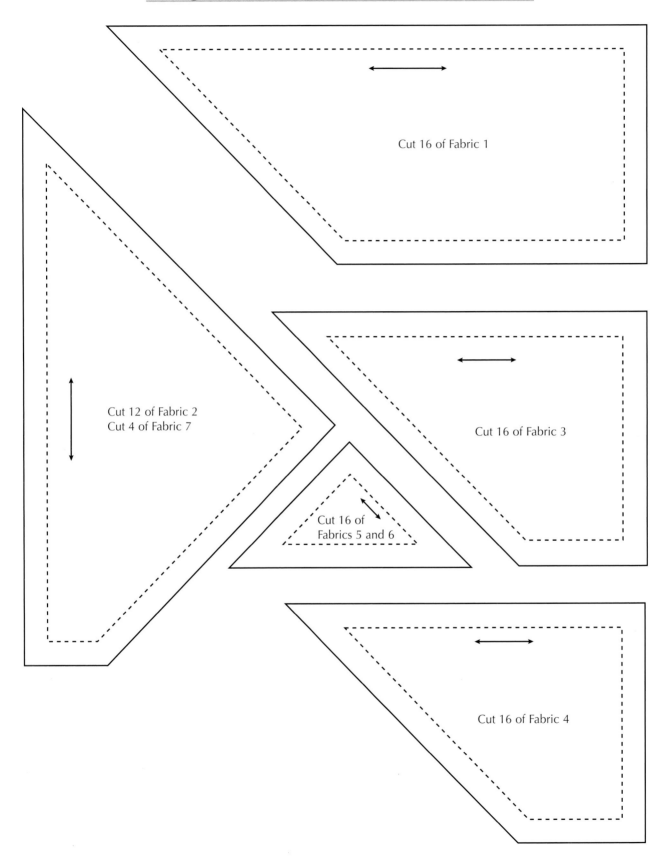

Cut 16 of Fabric 1

Cut 12 of Fabric 2
Cut 4 of Fabric 7

Cut 16 of Fabric 3

Cut 16 of
Fabrics 5 and 6

Cut 16 of Fabric 4

REFERENCE BOOKS

ON DESIGN AND COLOR

Perry, Gai. *Impressionist Quilts.* Lafayette, California: C&T Publishing, 1995.

Perry, Gai. *Impressionist Palette: Quilt Color & Design.* Lafayette, California: C&T Publishing, 1997.

Perry, Gai. *Color from the Heart.* Lafayette, California: C&T Publishing, 1999.

ON BASIC QUILTING TECHNIQUES

Fons, Marianne, and Liz Porter. *Quilter's Complete Guide.* Birmingham, Alabama: Oxmoor House, Inc., 1993.

Hargrave, Harriet, *Heirloom Machine Quilting.* Lafayette, California: C&T Publishing, 1995.

Hargrave, Harriet, and Sharyn Craig. *The Art of Classic Quiltmaking.* Lafayette, California: C&T Publishing, 1995.

Leone, Diana. *The New Sampler Quilt.* Lafayette, California: C&T Publishing, 1993.

McClun, Diana, and Laura Nownes. *Quilts, Quilts and More Quilts!* Lafayette, California: C&T Publishing, 1993.

INDEX

07/02
CWMARS

ABOUT THE AUTHOR

$\mathcal{G}$ai Perry began her romance with quilting in 1981, and she has been pursuing this passion ever since.

In 1985, Gai started teaching quiltmaking at local shops and seminars. Her fondness for antiques led her to focus on the effective use of color and fabric in traditional-style quilts. By 1990, she had a desire to start painting again, but instead of working with brushes, she developed an original style of quilting she called "The Art of the Impressionist Landscape." She has written two books on her techniques, *Impressionist Quilts* and *Impressionist Palette*.

Just for a change of pace, in 1999 Gai wrote *Color From the Heart*, a fascinating collection of traditional color and design lessons. Now, with the publication of her fourth book, Gai says she is intrigued with writing, and if she wasn't so involved with quilting, she would start her first novel.

For a complete list of books from C&T Publishing or for additional information, contact:

C&T Publishing, Inc.
P.O. Box 1456
Lafayette, CA 94549
(800) 284-1114
e-mail: ctinfo@ctpub.com
http://www.ctpub.com

For quilting supplies, contact:

The Cotton Patch Mail Order
3405 Hall Lane, Dept. CTB
Lafayette, CA 94549
(800) 835-4418
(925) 283-7883
e-mail: quiltusa@yahoo.com
http://www.quiltusa.com